The Power of Life and Death Is In Our Tongue

Diane Tanous

This book is dedicated to the body of Christ,
for whom Jesus gave His life
so that we could have
the overcoming power and victory
in our lives.

Contents

1

What was that - about the tongue?

Death and life are in the power of the tongue,
And those who love it will eat its fruit.

Prov 18:21 NASB

Words kill, words give life; they're either poison or
fruit—you choose.

Prov 18:21 TMT

The tongue can bring death or life; those who
love to talk will reap the consequences.

Prov 18:21 NLT

Words can bring death or life! Talk too much, and
you will eat everything you say.

Prov 18:21 CEV

The tongue has the power of life and death,
and those who love it will eat its fruit.

Prov 18:21 NIV

2

Do our words really have power?

From a surface perspective, we have all seen how the spoken word is very powerful to change a course of events in our own lives as well as on a world-wide scale. Words have been the cause of world wars. Harsh words can leave terrible scars on a child's soul and affect their behavior for life. Words can end marriages and cause affairs to begin. Kind words can lift spirits. Motivating words can cause victories. The media is all about putting words into people's ears and getting people believing one way or another. Words have an amazing power to solidify things that perhaps were still in question in our minds. Once we speak words – either positive or negative – they appear to be capable of bringing forth a physical manifestation of what we spoke– good or bad. The words we speak are heard and, once believed, can change the very direction of our lives.

From a scientific perspective, you can find many studies showing how prayer has positive effects on sick patients and on one's overall health. There have also, been studies showing the power of positive words and thoughts toward inanimate objects, such as water and food, and animate objects as well, such as animals and plants. One Scientific study has shown positive changes in water crystals at a molecular level through the power of kind words spoken to the water. Since our bodies are up to 60% water, negative words may be affecting our health more than we know.

From a biblical perspective, God's words have always been shown to have power. God formed this world through His spoken word. Isaiah says in the Bible that even though the grass withers and the flowers fade away, the Word of God will stand forever. In

Hebrews 4, it tells us that the Word of God is living and powerful and sharper than any two edged sword. In Isaiah, it says God's Word that goes forth from His mouth has the power to do what He sent it forth to do and will not return to Him void. Jesus was the Word made flesh. In Philippians 2, it says that speaking the name of Jesus has the power to cause every knee to bow on earth and in Heaven. It says that there is authority in the name of Jesus and that it can cause Demons to flee. With words, Jesus performed many miracles; He spoke and the dead were raised; He spoke and the wind and sea obeyed; He spoke and sick were healed; He spoke and gold coins manifested; He spoke and lives were changed forever. In the Old Testament, prophets and fathers could speak blessing or cursing over nations and children with words. In 1 Peter, it says that when we speak, we should speak as one speaking the very words of God. In Proverbs 15, it says that when we speak good things, it gives us life; however, when we speak perverseness, our spirits are crushed, and, as the title of this book suggests, life and death can be brought forth by the words we speak. So, if we believe in the Bible, we can safely assume that our words have some kind of power!

The Bible says the following about God's word:

"Is not my word like fire," declares the LORD, *"and like a hammer that breaks a rock in pieces?*
Jeremiah 23:29

So shall My word be that goes forth from My mouth; It shall not return to Me void, But it shall accomplish what I please, And it shall prosper in the thing for which I sent it.
Isaiah 55:11

It is the Spirit who gives life; the flesh profits nothing. The words that I speak to you are spirit, and they are life.
John 6:63

10

For the word of God is living and powerful, and sharper than any two-edged sword, piercing even to the division of soul and spirit, and of joints and marrow, and is a discerner of the thoughts and intents of the heart.

Hebrews 4:12

My son, give attention to my words; Incline your ear to my sayings. Do not let them depart from your eyes; Keep them in the midst of your heart; For they are life to those who find them, And health to all their flesh.

Proverbs 4:20-22

3

What is coming out of our mouths?

Have you ever just listened to yourself throughout the day? It is hard to do, but I successfully did it once while pretending I was being tape-recorded and that the tape was going to be heard over a loud speaker by the whole world that evening. Believe me, I caught and changed my words and tone a lot that day! I was doing it in an effort to see what I sounded like to my family. You see, there had been complaints about my tone and nagging at which I would retort, "I do NOT sound like that!" I would challenge us as Bible believing Christians to try this exercise with the exception that every time we speak, Jesus and the angels are standing in the room. I wonder what would remain unsaid and what would be spoken for all of heaven to hear?

Shouldn't we, the church, be sounding different than the world? After all, we ARE the body of Christ. Should the body of Christ be doubting, fearing, judging, grumbling, complaining, despairing, disputing, panicking, cursing, or gossiping? I don't think that was what the "good tidings of great joy" was supposed to produce. I think God is trying to tell us that He has given us everything we need for victory – go ahead - proclaim it and act on it. Yes, we, the body of Christ, should sound different than the world.

You are of God, little children, and have overcome them, because He who is in you is greater than he who is in the world. They are of the world. Therefore they speak as of the world, and the world hears them. We are of God.

1 John 4:4-6

Do all things without complaining and disputing, that you may become blameless and harmless, children of God without fault in the midst of a crooked and perverse generation, among whom you shine as lights in the world, holding fast the word of life, so that I may rejoice in the day of Christ that I have not run in vain or labored in vain.

Philippians 2:14-16

The way of the wicked is like darkness; They do not know what makes them stumble. My son, give attention to my words; Incline your ear to my sayings. Do not let them depart from your eyes; Keep them in the midst of your heart; For they are life to those who find them, And health to all their flesh. Keep your heart with all diligence, For out of it spring the issues of life. Put away from you a deceitful mouth, and put perverse lips far from you.

Proverbs 4:20-24

Do not conform any longer to the pattern of this world, but be transformed by the renewing of your mind. Then you will be able to test and approve what God's will is—his good, pleasing and perfect will.

Romans 12:2

So I tell you this, and insist on it in the Lord, that you must no longer live as the Gentiles do, in the futility of their thinking. They are darkened in their understanding and separated from the life of God because of the ignorance that is in them due to the hardening of their hearts.

Ephesians 4:17-18

*Let no one deceive you with empty words, for because
of these things the wrath of God comes upon the sons
of disobedience. Therefore do not be partakers with
them.*

Ephesians 5:6-7

If you asked someone, "If given a choice, would you purposefully curse or bless your life?" What do you think their response would be? Personally, I would bless my life. Well, do you know that many of us curse ourselves with our words all day long? With words of doubt, grumbling, fear, judgment, negativity, and defeat. Words that line up with the world, unbelievers, and the devil. Words that, I believe, if Jesus were here, he would marvel at... Words like: " 'I'm so afraid...', 'my situation is killing me', 'I'll pray but I don't expect much', 'God must hate me', 'God must want me sick', 'I fear I have cancer', 'my arthritis', 'my diabetes', 'the doctor says it's fatal', 'I don't love my spouse anymore', 'I'm afraid I'm going to lose my job', 'I am sick and tired', 'I'm depressed', 'I'm no good', 'I could never do that', 'that makes me crazy', 'I'm losing my mind', 'I guess God doesn't want to heal me', 'I guess it worked for them but not for me', 'I've been this way my whole life and this is how I'll die', 'I cannot quit', 'I've lost everything', 'I don't want to live anymore', 'I don't deserve that', 'I could never do that', 'It's all your fault', 'that child is hopeless', 'I wouldn't survive without health insurance', 'I feel tired all the time', 'I can't ever get ahead...'" and on and on it goes.

Word curses are bad enough coming from other people into our souls, but we should be careful not to curse our own lives with careless words that give the enemy rights to do his work.

If you have ever been around a person who complains a lot, you're probably aware that it can begin to affect us negatively. It not only is poisoning their soul with sin, but it begins to rub off on our soul. Sometimes it has a ripple effect. I have managed to get my whole family in a bad mood just by complaining. It poisons the atmosphere and makes us physically tired. When we grumble and complain, I believe it affects us spiritually and physically and needs

15

to be repented of quickly. God's Word lets us know that He is not pleased with it. Grumbling should not be part of a Christian's personality. When our teens grumble, we need to turn it around quickly before it becomes a negative habit that will poison their lives and the lives of others around them. Train our children to have thankful hearts, not grumbling hearts.

The Bible lets us know what God thinks about grumbling and complaining:

> *...nor let us tempt Christ, as some of them also tempted, and were destroyed by serpents; nor complain, as some of them also complained, and were destroyed by the destroyer. Now all these things happened to them as examples, and they were written for our admonition, upon whom the ends of the ages have come.*
>
> 1 Corinthians 10:9-11

> *Do all things without complaining and disputing, that you may become blameless and harmless, children of God without fault in the midst of a crooked and perverse generation, among whom you shine as lights in the world, holding fast the word of life, so that I may rejoice in the day of Christ that I have not run in vain or labored in vain.*
>
> Philippians 2:14-15

> *Do not grumble against one another, brethren, lest you be condemned. Behold, the Judge is standing at the door!*
>
> James 5:9

> *A fool's mouth is his destruction, and his lips are the snare of his soul.*
>
> Proverbs 18:7

The Bible clearly instructs us about what should and shouldn't be coming out of our mouths!

The good man brings good things out of the good stored up in him, and the evil man brings evil things out of the evil stored up in him. But I tell you that men will have to give account on the day of judgment for every careless word they have spoken. For by your words you will be acquitted, and by your words you will be condemned."

Matthew 12:35-37

A man's stomach shall be satisfied from the fruit of his mouth; From the produce of his lips he shall be filled.

Proverbs 18:20

A wholesome tongue is a tree of life, but perverseness in it breaks the spirit.

Proverbs 15:4

"Their throat is an open tomb; With their tongues they have practiced deceit. The poison of asps is under their lips. Whose mouth is full of cursing and bitterness."

Romans 3:13-14

When He had called the multitude to Himself, He said to them, "Hear and understand: Not what goes into the mouth defiles a man; but what comes out of the mouth, this defiles a man."

Matthew 15:10-11

But no man can tame the tongue. It is an unruly evil, full of deadly poison. With it we bless our God and Father, and with it we curse men, who have been

*made in the similitude of God. Out of the same mouth
proceed blessing and cursing. My brethren, these
things ought not to be so.*

James 3:8-10

*For the foolish person will speak foolishness, And
his heart will work iniquity: To practice ungodliness,
To utter error against the LORD, To keep the hungry
unsatisfied, And he will cause the drink of the thirsty
to fail.*

Isaiah 32:6

*And the tongue is a fire, a world of iniquity. The
tongue is so set among our members that it defiles the
whole body, and sets on fire the course of nature; and
it is set on fire by hell.*

James 3:6

*For he who would love life And see good days, Let
him refrain his tongue from evil, And his lips from
speaking deceit.*

1Peter 3:10

*Let no corrupt word proceed out of your mouth, but
what is good for necessary edification, that it may
impart grace to the hearers. And do not grieve the
Holy Spirit of God, by whom you were sealed for the
day of redemption. Let all bitterness, wrath, anger,
clamor, and evil speaking be put away from you, with
all malice.*

Ephesians 4:29-30

*All Your works shall praise You, O LORD, And Your
saints shall bless You. They shall SPEAK of the glory
of Your kingdom, And TALK of Your power, To make*

known to the sons of men His mighty acts, And the glorious majesty of His kingdom.

Psalm 145:10-12

Let my mouth be filled with Your praise And with Your glory all the day.

Psalm 71:8

And my tongue shall sing aloud of Your righteousness. O Lord, open my lips, And my mouth shall show forth Your praise.

Psalm 51:14-15

For my mouth will speak truth; Wickedness is an abomination to my lips.

Proverbs 8:7

Let the redeemed of the LORD say so, Whom He has redeemed from the hand of the enemy...

Psalm 107:2

Let the weak say, 'I am strong.'

Joel 3:10

I said to myself, "I will watch what I do and not sin in what I say. I will hold my tongue when the ungodly are around me."

Psalm 39:1

For with the heart one believes unto righteousness, and with the mouth confession is made unto salvation.

Romans 10:10

...to speak evil of no one, to be peaceable, gentle, showing all humility to all men.

Titus 3:2

19

...If anyone speaks, he should do it as one speaking the very words of God...

1Peter 4:10

but, speaking the truth in love, may grow up in all things into Him who is the head—Christ—

Ephesians 4:15

speaking to one another in psalms and hymns and spiritual songs, singing and making melody in your heart to the Lord,...

Ephesians 5:19

...let it not even be named among you, as is fitting for saints; neither filthiness, nor foolish talking, nor coarse jesting, which are not fitting, but rather giving of thanks.

Ephesians 5:3-4

Because Your loving kindness is better than life, My lips shall praise You.

Psalm 63:3

Oh, give thanks to the LORD! Call upon His name; Make known His deeds among the peoples! Sing to Him, sing psalms to Him; Talk of all His wondrous works!

Psalm 105:1-2

4

Our mouths beg the question: Do we "believers" actually believe God's word?

"Well everyone doubts a little," you may be thinking. This is what fighting the fight of faith is all about – dispersing doubt. However, doubting is very serious business in a life that depends on faith. It says in Hebrews that, without faith, it is impossible to please God. Doubt is the tool that Satan and our own minds use to keep us from having victory in this Christian life we have chosen to live. James says,

> *But let him ask in faith, with no doubting, for he who doubts is like a wave of the sea driven and tossed by the wind. For let not that man suppose that he will receive anything from the Lord; he is a double-minded man, unstable in all his ways.*
>
> James 1:6-8

Hmmm... Double minded? Unstable?

Does the church seem a little unstable and double minded at times -speaking out fear and doubt ? Speaking less than what God has said begins with unbelief and/or ignorance in our hearts of what God has told us He will do and out of the overflow of our hearts our mouths have spoken.

I have heard stories from "Christians" (including myself) of woe and doom and grumbling and complaining, and I sit there as my family in Christ describes marital woes, teen woes, sickness woes,

21

financial woes, but not with a sense of having victory, but more with a sense of hopelessness, with a sense of fear, a sense that they have no say in the matter, or with a sort of acceptance. Sometimes I will sit and think -- "Ye of little faith – have you not read what God did for you in your Bible recently?" In the New Testament, the enemy doesn't have much authority except for what we give him. We wonder, "How did we get here?" I would challenge us to look and ask – "What was my MOUTH doing (or not doing) when the economy started getting strained? What was my mouth doing (or not doing) when symptoms of disease started pounding at my body? What was my mouth doing (or not doing) when my children were in their pre-teens? What was my mouth doing (or not doing) when I noticed my spouse veering off the straight path? What were we speaking or not speaking out over our family and our circumstances? Blessing or cursing? Life or death? Were we praising or grumbling? Praying or sighing? Remember, Proverbs 26:2 tells us that a curse does not come without a cause. Granted, some trials seemingly jump on us with no warning, but even then, a dose of God's Word (our sword) is enough to begin the good fight of faith.

My husband said to me one day when I was being wishy-washy in my faith, "God's either God or He's not!" I needed to hear those words! They hit me like a brick; because when I thought about it, I realized that I was really doubting God. This puts us, His people, on very shaky ground that the enemy can pull out from under us. Some of us will defend the Bible theologically as truth over and over again, but yet when presented with certain circumstances, you'd never think we had read it. Our mouths can reflect unbelief daily. In one day, we can speak more unbelief than the world. When he was in his prime, even Mohammad Ali knew the effects of speaking victory over his life. Go ahead... Look in the mirror and say "I AM RE-DEEMED!" "I HAVE VICTORY THROUGH CHRIST!" "YOUR WORD IS TRUE, LORD AND I BELIEVE IT!" "YOU ARE BIGGER THAN MY PROBLEMS!"

"And when the LORD saw it, He spurned them, Because of the provocation of His sons and His daughters. And He said: 'I will hide My face from them, I will see what their end will be, For they are a perverse generation, Children in whom is no faith. They have provoked Me to jealousy by what is not God; They have moved Me to anger by their foolish idols.

Deuteronomy 32:19-21

"He healed me before, but this is much worse...!"

When Peter began to sink, the Bible says,

...And immediately Jesus stretched out His hand and caught him, and said to him, "O you of little faith, why did you doubt?"

Matthew 14:31

To me, Jesus is saying, "Peter you already saw that I could do it; why did you let those waves scare you out of believing my abilities?" Do you think Jesus is saying to us, "You have read and seen what I have done in the past for you and others; do you think this situation is now too big for me?"

Nothing is impossible for our God – He created the universe, for Heaven's sake! God has always been a God of the unusual and impossible. Jesus knows who His Father is and so should we.

Then Abraham fell on his face and laughed, and said in his heart, "Shall a child be born to a man who is one hundred years old? And shall Sarah, who is ninety years old, bear a child?"

Genesis 17:17

When Jesus came into the ruler's house, and saw the flute players and the noisy crowd wailing, He said to

23

them, "Make room, for the girl is not dead, but sleeping." And they ridiculed Him. But when the crowd was put outside, He went in and took her by the hand, and the girl arose.

Matthew 9:23-25

Remember David when He went to feed his brothers in the army? When circumstances brought him face to face with the giant that had the whole army "dismayed and greatly afraid," what did David do?

Then David said to the Philistine, "You come to me with a sword, with a spear, and with a javelin. But I come to you in the name of the LORD of hosts, the God of the armies of Israel, whom you have defied. This day the LORD will deliver you into my hand, and I will strike you and take your head from you. And this day I will give the carcasses of the camp of the Philistines to the birds of the air and the wild beasts of the earth, that all the earth may know that there is a God in Israel. Then all this assembly shall know that the LORD does not save with sword and spear; for the battle is the LORD's, and He will give you into our hands."

1Samuel 17:45-47

David spoke to the giant in his life and proclaimed his victory! Why? Because he knew who his God was and had complete faith in what He could and would do. David spoke like a child of God to the problem that had threatened his family, and what he spoke was then manifested because he believed in his God. David saw the victory already won! If Goliath represents the stronghold of every problem that can attack a Christian (financial, relational, emotional, physical), do you think we could be more like David, instead of the rest of the army, and declare what our God can do, will do, and has already done?

24

"When the going gets tough, the tough do what?"

*And a great windstorm arose, and the waves beat
into the boat, so that it was already filling. But He
was in the stern, asleep on a pillow. And they awoke
Him and said to Him, "Teacher, do You not care that
we are perishing?" Then He arose and rebuked the
wind, and said to the sea, "Peace, be still!" And the
wind ceased and there was a great calm. But He said
to them, "Why are you so fearful? How is it that you
have no faith?" And they feared exceedingly, and
said to one another, "Who can this be, that even the
wind and the sea obey Him!"*

Mark 4:37-41

Do we panic when things get too visual? When the storm came
the disciples panicked and began to wonder if God cared that they
were perishing! Jesus already knew God's will, God's word, God's
authority, and God's love. He was not moved by the visual severity
of the storm and calmed the situation with His words. Do you think
that we look at the obvious signs of sickness or dire circumstances
and, because of what we see, begin to question if God even cares
that we could be perishing? Do we doubt His love for us? What
do you think Jesus is saying to us when we do that? Perhaps he is
asking – "Why are you so fearful? Do you not know that I love you
with an undying love? These symptoms are nothing to me. How
is it that you have no faith?" If Jesus is the same today, yesterday,
and forever, shouldn't we be able to take in a sigh of relief and say,
"Although it looks bad, I know you have given me the victory and I
will rejoice!"

Also, take note that the disciples also feared when he calmed
the storm. If we would be in faith to visualize the victory before
it happened, wouldn't that be helpful towards getting that victory?

25

Instead, we spend so much time focused on the problem that we are shocked when the miracle happens. Then, the first thing out of our mouth is, "Oh my God, I can't believe I'm healed!"

Maybe we should practice visualizing the victory so we won't be focused on the storm and so shocked when victory comes!

"But that was Jesus..."

Have you ever heard anyone say, "Yeah, but that was Jesus...?" Do you realize that one reason He came was to make us like him? Paul and the disciples of Jesus gave proof that "average" people could do what He did. We have the same Holy Spirit power in us. Jesus came to bring us back to our Father and to put us into a position to be overcomers in this life through the Holy Spirit. He wants us to be a church operating in obedience, power, love, and faith. Jesus himself made the comment:

> *"Most assuredly, I say to you, he who believes in Me, the works that I do he will do also; and greater works than these he will do, because I go to My Father.*
> John 14:12

> *...and what is the exceeding greatness of His power toward us who believe, according to the working of His mighty power which He worked in Christ when He raised Him from the dead and seated Him at His right hand in the heavenly places,...*
> Ephesians 1:19-20

> *Therefore, having these promises, beloved, let us cleanse ourselves from all filthiness of the flesh and spirit, perfecting holiness in the fear of God.*
> 2 Corinthians 7:1

Heal the sick, cleanse the lepers, raise the dead, cast out demons. Freely you have received, freely give.

Matthew 10:8

For we are His workmanship, created in Christ Jesus for good works, which God prepared beforehand that we should walk in them.

Ephesians 2:10

He who overcomes shall inherit all things, and I will be his God and he shall be My son.

Revelations 21:7

And these signs will accompany those who believe: In my name they will drive out demons; they will speak in new tongues; they will pick up snakes with their hands; and when they drink deadly poison, it will not hurt them at all; they will place their hands on sick people, and they will get well."

Mark 16:17-18 NIV

We are God's children, adopted heirs with Christ. Jesus believed in His Father – shouldn't we? Jesus said trials and tribulations would come, but how does he want us to react? He says "...be of good cheer..." "How can we be of good cheer?" one might ask. The good cheer can come because no matter what happens, we are promised victory through Jesus Christ and what He accomplished. Everything Jesus did on this earth was for our victory. He became a curse for us so we would not have to be cursed. He was wounded for our transgressions, chastised to give us peace, and by his stripes, we were healed. Jesus overcame. He overcame the world, the devil, the flesh, and even death itself so we could have victory. He went away so that we could be filled with the power from the Holy Spirit and walk in His fruits and gifts. Now all we have to do is receive this gift of life and begin walking in who he said we are and in what He has provided.

"Well, that's just not realistic..."

We are human and being realistic (expressing an awareness of things as they are) is only natural. But our God is a God of the supernatural: creation, Abraham, Moses, Noah's ark, the Exodus, Jonah, Jericho, Gideon, Elijah, Paul, Peter, etc... Jesus seems to be asking us to step above the natural and see things in the supernatural.

> *"Do not be afraid; only believe."*
>
> Mark 5:36

> *And Jesus answered and said to them, "Truly I say to you, if you have faith and do not doubt, you will not only do what was done to the fig tree, but even if you say to this mountain, 'Be taken up and cast into the sea,' it will happen. "And all things you ask in prayer, believing, you will receive."*
>
> Matthew 21:21-22

And again, He said in Mark,

> *"Have faith in God. For assuredly, I say to you, whoever says to this mountain, 'Be removed and be cast into the sea,' and does not doubt in his heart, but believes that those things he says will be done, he will have whatever he says. Therefore I say to you, whatever things you ask when you pray, believe that you receive them, and you will have them.*
>
> Mark 11:23-24

Do you think that God is trying to tell us that no natural circumstances should hinder our faith in what He can do, and that, if we would open the doors to faith, He can do mighty things? But if we fear and doubt, the enemy will step in to attack us. Perhaps the enemy couldn't get us so steeped in dire straits if, long before the circumstances occurred, we had trusted in God, meditated on His word, practiced a righteous mouth, and spoke forth His life over ourselves.

I tell you, he will see that they get justice, and quickly.
However, when the Son of Man comes, will he find
faith on the earth?"

Luke 18:8

Examine yourselves as to whether you are in the faith.
Test yourselves. Do you not know yourselves, that
Jesus Christ is in you? — unless indeed you are
disqualified.

2Corinthians 13:5

"Excuse me Lord; I have only been attending church for 18 years..."

I sat in church for years agreeing with the words taught, learning the powerful promises made to me from God, and learning about my authority. But when I went home, it hadn't really changed me much. I was still in control. My prayer life wasn't that great because I was doing a "good" job holding everything together on my own. But when a crisis hit (and it did), instead of trusting in Him and putting to use all that He had been trying to tell me, I gave way to doubt and fear and had a near-nervous breakdown. How long will it take us to believe in what Jesus has done for us and begin to put it into action? How long before we trust that He loves us and wants the best for us?

"But why do you call Me 'Lord, Lord,' and not do the
things which I say?"

Luke 6:46

Remember Judas – a "chosen" one? He was one of Jesus' intimates and heard everything Jesus spoke; he ate with Jesus and witnessed his miracles Yet, his heart was not sold out. Instead, Judas sold out Jesus for thirty pieces of silver. How many of us attend church on Sunday, know the Bible inside and out, but still take control and live for our own agendas? Remember, Jesus said that we who love our lives will lose them, but if we lose "our lives" for His

29

sake we will find life. In Proverbs it says, trust in the LORD with all your heart and lean not on your own understanding. We need to know that God wants to relationship with us so we can know His will and be overcomers.

Also, remember the Israelites and God's plan to move them to a wonderful promised land. They were God's people and God had wonderful plans for them. What happened in the desert, anyway? Discomfort; Doubt; Fear; They forgot everything God had just done on their behalf. Then, from the overflow of their hearts, their mouths began to speak -- and what did they say? They spoke against Moses. They spoke of lack – they spoke their doubt, fear, and discomfort. He describes them in Hebrews as "a stiff necked people". Through their stubbornness, they brought a curse on themselves; their doubts in God's love for them kept them from receiving God's fullest blessing of the promise.

In Exodus 17, the Bible tells us

> *"...the people thirsted there for water, and the people complained against Moses, and said, 'Why is it you have brought us up out of Egypt, to kill us and our children and our livestock with thirst?' "*
>
> Exodus 17:3

Take note that their grumbling came after the ten plagues (that did not touch them), the parting of the Red Sea, the bitter water turned sweet, the manna, and their song of praise to the Lord for deliverance straight out of the Egyptians' hands. How could those Israelites be so forgetful and so faithless after all God did for them? Well, I wonder if Jesus is saying "How can My body be so forgetful and faithless after all I've done for them? "

> *For if these things are yours and abound, you will be neither barren nor unfruitful in the knowledge of our Lord Jesus Christ. For he who lacks these things is shortsighted, even to blindness, and has forgotten that he was cleansed from his old sins.*
>
> 2 Peter 1:8-9

Jesus' work on the cross covered it all , and yet, some of us are still living lukewarm, mediocre, and grumbling lives; grumbling about our lives, our families, or our pastors instead of praying for them; living like the world, talking like the world, and trusting in worldly wisdom. Trusting in doctors' reports, healthcare, government, money, insurance, drugs, and idols, instead of trusting the glorious God who can deliver us through all trials!

Are we not living under a new and better covenant as stated in Hebrews 8:6? We have to be careful of the sin of unbelief. It is unbelief in what He says that ends us up in distressing places where the enemy can torment us in our minds. Remember all of His glorious promises. Have we not been promised life and life more abundantly? Have we not been promised to have everything we need to live a life of godliness? Have we not been promised our sins forgiven? Are we not promised in James that the prayer of faith will heal the sick? Were we not healed by His stripes mentioned three times in Isaiah, Matthew, and Peter? Did He not tell us that he hates divorce? Did not Jeremiah and Paul say that God knows us and has good plans for us – not for harm, but to prosper us? Did he not say in Mark 11:23 that if we do not doubt but believe, we will have anything we say? Did Jesus not say to be of good cheer because He has overcome the world? Did He not say that we overcome the world through our faith? Did He not say to trust in him with all our heart? Did He not say: do not fear, be not afraid, do not be anxious for anything, do not fear what they fear, do not worry about tomorrow? Did He not say that the same power that raised Christ from the dead lives in us? Did He not say ask and you will receive? Did He not say how much more would the father in heaven give good gifts to those who ask? Did He not say we were redeemed from the curse because He became a curse for us? Did He not say that He is the God Who heals us, and that He sent His word to heal us and deliver us from all destruction?

What if we just sold out to this gospel message? Well, to sell out and "only believe" might mean that we would begin to hear more praise and thanksgiving out of our mouths instead of grumbling and complaining. It would mean that we would love and obey Him. It would mean that we would be baptized in the Holy Spirit and find peace and victory through trials and tribulations. It may mean that we would lay hands on the sick and watch them recover; it may mean that we would cast out demons, raise the dead, or pray in tongues. We would begin walking in our calling, in sincere love, building others up, prophesying life over our families, and living a life revealing the fruits of the Holy Spirit. Let's face it – the church might become a peculiar people!

For this is the love of God, that we keep His commandments. And His commandments are not burdensome. For whatever is born of God overcomes the world. And this is the victory that has overcome the world—our faith.

1 John 5:3-4

But thanks be to God, who gives us the victory through our Lord Jesus Christ. Therefore, my beloved brethren, be steadfast, immovable, always abounding in the work of the Lord, knowing that your labor is not in vain in the Lord.

1 Corinthians 15:57-58

So he gave them his attention, expecting to receive something from them. Then Peter said, "Silver and gold I do not have, but what I do have I give you: In the name of Jesus Christ of Nazareth, rise up and walk." And he took him by the right hand and lifted him up, and immediately his feet and ankle bones received strength.

Acts 3:5-7

5

Do we have an enemy trying to get us to doubt God's word?

It is worth mentioning that we do have an enemy; but some of us give no thought to Satan and his demons, even though Jesus spent a good portion of His ministry casting them out of the sick and oppressed – He was even tempted by Satan himself. One helpful strategy in a fight (of faith) is to know our enemy and know how he operates!

"WHAT? You mean the devil is real?"

Yes, he is real. In John 12, Jesus calls him the "ruler of this world." Peter says in 1 Peter 5:8-9,

> *"Be sober, be vigilant; because your adversary the devil walks about like a roaring lion, seeking whom he may devour. Resist him, steadfast in the faith, knowing that the same sufferings are experienced by your brotherhood in the world."*

Jesus describes our enemy again in John 8:44. He says to the Pharisees,

> *"You are of your father the devil, and the desires of your father you want to do. He was a murderer from the beginning, and does not stand in the truth, because there is no truth in him. When he speaks a lie, he speaks from his own resources, for he is a liar and the father of it."*

What was the serpent's tactic when speaking to Eve in the garden? He was trying to get her to doubt what God had said. His first attack on God's creation was to get them to doubt God's word. And remember, doubt always precedes fear or pride.

> And he said to the woman, "Has God indeed said, 'You shall not eat of every tree of the garden'?" And the woman said to the serpent, "We may eat the fruit of the trees of the garden; but of the fruit of the tree which is in the midst of the garden, God has said, 'You shall not eat it, nor shall you touch it, lest you die.'" Then the serpent said to the woman, "You will not surely die... "
>
> Genesis 3:1-4

If the enemy can succeed in getting us to doubt God's word, then our sword, our breastplate, our shield, our helmet, our belt, and our shoes have been compromised! Paul says in Ephesians 6 that we need this armor because

> "...we do not wrestle against flesh and blood, but against principalities, against powers, against the rulers of the darkness of this age, against spiritual hosts of wickedness in the heavenly places."
>
> Ephesians 6:12

We are in a spiritual battle whether we like it or not. The difference is that some know it and others do not. Some of us are standing against him and engaging with our swords (God's word) and others are not. Our lack of action is like someone announcing that the enemy was coming and we all just sat down, put our swords on the ground, took our armor off, and began to sleep.

Is it any wonder that many in the church are sick, panicked, depressed, on drugs, stressed, or burned out? They don't even know that they have an enemy who has been working since the creation of the Garden of Eden to get them to believe something other than what God spoke, including the thought that there is no enemy. Should God's people know the truth, this truth would set them free from the things that are keeping them from spiritual, mental, and physical victory?

Ignorance is not bliss for us...

Remember that lack of knowledge of His word can mean defeat:

My people are destroyed for lack of knowledge. Because you have rejected knowledge, I also will reject you from being priest for Me; Because you have forgotten the law of your God, I also will forget your children.

Hosea 4:6

Be diligent to present yourself approved to God, a worker who does not need to be ashamed, rightly dividing the word of truth. But shun profane and idle babblings, for they will increase to more ungodliness.

2 Timothy 2:15-16

6

Be of good cheer because Jesus gave us ways to overcome this lying enemy and be overcomers!

Not only do we have His Word to attack , we have the word of our testimony and authority in the Name of Jesus to overcome the enemy and to come against his lies, and our shield of faith to extinguish his fiery darts (Note: this requires our mouths to speak).

Then the seventy returned with joy, saying, "Lord, even the demons are subject to us in Your name."

Luke 10:17

"Behold, I have given you authority to tread on serpents and scorpions, and over all the power of the enemy, and nothing will injure you.

Luke 10:19

And they overcame him by the blood of the Lamb and by the word of their testimony, and they did not love their lives to the death.

Revelation 12:11

... and having shod your feet with the preparation of the gospel of peace; above all, taking the shield of faith with which you will be able to quench all the fiery darts of the wicked one. And take the helmet of

37

salvation, and the sword of the Spirit, which is the
word of God; praying always with all prayer and
supplication in the Spirit, being watchful to this end
with all perseverance and supplication for all the
saints

Ephesians 6:15-18

Jesus used the Scriptures when He was tempted in the desert by Satan. He used His sword and His shield.

And the devil said to Him, "If You are the Son of God,
command this stone to become bread." But Jesus an-
swered him, saying, "It is written, 'Man shall not live
by bread alone, but by every word of God. "

Luke 4:3-4

Remember when Jesus drove the people out who were defiling the temple of the Lord? Guess what? We are the temple now, and even though God's Holy Spirit abides in the inner holy place, demons can reside in our outer court (our soul), defiling and/or oppressing us. He said:

If anyone defiles the temple of God, God will destroy
him. For the temple of God is holy, which temple you
are.

1 Corinthians 3:17

I think Jesus was giving us an example to keep our minds praying, kept pure, and to drive out the demonic influences that contaminate our temples.

Why would we – covered by His blood and being armed with the very name that every knee shall bow to – let the enemy run wild over us or our children? Remember the epileptic boy who was being thrown into the fire and water; do you remember Jesus' words when he came to the father? He said,"You wicked and perverse generation, how much longer do I have to put up with you?" Why do you think he said that?

I think what Jesus is trying to tell us is this: through prayer, fasting, and His name, we have complete authority. Why do we put up with and quietly accept the devil's lies and sicknesses when Jesus gives us authority to get him out of our lives and our children's lives? I think Jesus and His angels marvel at our inactivity against the lies of the enemy! He's got nothing on a believer except for what we give him through our lack of obedience, lack of faith, and ignorance of the word.

What if, when sickness is trying to overtake our bodies, instead of listening to the spirit of fear and lying on our back, we stood up and pulled out God's lovely sword and said, "Satan, you are a liar. I resist your lies and attack. It is written that I was healed by Jesus' stripes. I believe that I receive that healing now. I confess my sins and God is faithful and just to forgive me of them. I curse you virus, and command you to go in the name of Jesus. I command you, demon of infirmity, to get your hands off of me and get out of my house in the name of Jesus. He is my healer, and in Him do I trust. It is written that no pestilence shall overcome me. It is written that with long life He will satisfy me. He is the God that heals me. I praise you, Jesus, for your wonderful mercies. I praise you for the victory I have through Christ!" Then proceed to really upset the devil and start praising God with thanksgiving and shouting God's promises of victory!

For though we walk in the flesh, we do not war according to the flesh. For the weapons of our warfare are not carnal but mighty in God for pulling down strongholds, casting down arguments and every high thing that exalts itself against the knowledge of God, bringing every thought into captivity to the obedience of Christ,...

2 Corinthians 10:3-5

When stuff comes up against us that we know does not line up with what God's Word is speaking about, tell the enemy that you are the temple of God and that he is a liar and IT IS WRITTEN...!!

"Does that mean that I have to memorize scripture?"

Well, it is hard to wield your sword if you don't have one. Write the promises from the Bible down that pertain to your situation. There are some included at the end of this book. The more you read them and speak them, the more you'll remember them. God and His Word are powerful, and there are many ways to use the words that God has spoken. Praise is a mighty weapon, and God inhabits our praises and there is healing in His presence. Demons cannot easily attack a person who is praising God!

It is a good time for us to open our Bibles and see who we really are and what Jesus has done for us and to begin proclaiming life with our mouths. There is power in speaking the Word of God! It brings us life, health, and edifies others. Let's put the power of life back on our tongue and we will reap the rewards.

7

Brief Summary:

The words we speak do have power in them – power to have positive or negative effects on our lives.

Yes, as the body of Christ, we should sound (speak) different than the world.

Yes, many of us are living in doubt of God's very word, and this is reflected in our mouth because, from the overflow of the heart, the mouth speaks.

Yes, we do have an enemy whose goal is to get us to doubt God's word and lose our overcoming victory.

Yes, there is reason to rejoice: God has given us His Word! Through His word and the name of Jesus, He has given us authority over the enemy, circumstances, and our flesh. He has given us victory through faith in His Word. If we speak His Word, we will be putting the power of life back on our tongues.

8

The Many Blessings of Meditating on, Speaking, Singing, and Proclaiming God's Life Words over Ourselves, our Families, and our Circumstances

Then Jesus said to those Jews who believed Him,"If you abide in My word, you are My disciples indeed. And you shall know the truth, and the truth shall make you free."

John 8:31-32

1 –Speaking God's Word can help our faith grow.

One way we can help our faith grow (and our doubt shrink) is to speak God's truths into our lives and over our circumstances, instead of fear and doubt words.

Speak, speak, speak. Faith comes by what? - hearing and hearing the word of God. So let your mind hear what your mouth is speaking, and make sure your mouth is speaking truth from the Word of God.

So then faith comes by hearing, and hearing by the word of God.

Romans 10:17

43

Why do you think God changed Abram's very name from Abram to Abraham? What was he doing? By changing his name, he would now have to hear "father of many nations" over and over again. He would not be able to forget God's promise to Him. And note, God called him father of many nations before he even had one son.

> *No longer shall your name be called Abram, but your name shall be Abraham; for I have made you a father of many nations.*
>
> Genesis 17:5

What would happen if, instead of hearing "I am cursed with this condition," you heard, "I am blessed through the redemptive work of Jesus! Thank you, Lord, I am redeemed!!"

2 –Speaking God's truths helps us renew our minds and take thoughts captive.

The more we speak God's Word, the more we will begin noticing thoughts that don't line up with God's Word. Hearing it definitely helps us to take inventory of bad recordings that play in our heads that are not of God. By speaking God's word over our situations, it helps train our minds to listen to God's wisdom instead of the world's wisdom.

> *Do not conform any longer to the pattern of this world, but be transformed by the renewing of your mind. Then you will be able to test and approve what God's will is—his good, pleasing and perfect will.*
>
> Romans 12:2

> *We demolish arguments and every pretension that sets itself up against the knowledge of God, and we take captive every thought to make it obedient to Christ.*
>
> 2 Corinthians 10:5

3 –Speaking God's truths helps us overcome fear of the bad reports we hear all day.

We have to speak it; just to hear it on Sunday and agree with it is not enough. Our minds are bombarded daily with words of fear about natural disasters, epidemics, terrorists, and economic downturns. These come by way of radio, television, computer, newspapers, and other media, as well as other people. When our mouths are quiet, our minds ponder the "what if's ." Then, in comes the spirit of fear who compounds the situation with detailed scenarios of death and destruction. God tells us to think on only edifying things so that the enemy cannot so easily lure us into fear. These, in turn, should be the good reports we speak about, instead of the bad reports from the world.

And now, dear brothers and sisters, one final thing
- Fix your thoughts on what is true, and honorable,
and right, and pure, and lovely, and admirable. Think
about things that are excellent and worthy of praise.

Philippians 4:8

4 –Speaking God's Word over ourselves helps us not fall for the lies whispered to us by the enemy.

The enemy suggests to us lies that, if we are not careful, we will ponder on (and end up speaking out) instead of God's truths. We may even go so far as to believe the lie over the truth.

But when Jesus turned and looked at his disciples, he
rebuked Peter. "Get behind me, Satan!" he said. "You
do not have in mind the things of God, but the things
of men."

Mark 8:33

45

...Because you are strong, and the word of God abides
in you, And you have overcome the wicked one.

1John 2:14

When our mouths begin to practice God's truths, the enemy's whispers won't be accepted as easily! Praise and focusing on God's goodness literally starve the enemy right out of your life.

What if, every day when we woke up and our circumstances try to play over in our heads, we would just say out loud, "God, You are big enough to take care of this! I believe Who You say You are and Your promises are true!"

If we have a particular situation where we feel in defeat or in a battle, find the scriptures of promise, write them out, and put them on your mirror or all around your house to remind you of who you are and what you have in Christ, what God has promised you, and what Christ did for you on the cross. Speak them everyday like medicine and renew your mind by taking every thought captive unto Christ so that unbelief, ignorance, doubt, and the lies of the enemy will be replaced with faith, knowledge, hope, and truth.

5 -Speaking God's truths helps
to keep us spiritually minded.

Our flesh and carnal-mindedness can constantly plague us with ungodly desires which war against our very souls. We need to keep our minds on things of the spirit.

For to be carnally minded is death, but to be spiritu-
ally minded is life and peace.

Romans 8:6

Dear friends, I urge you, as aliens and strangers in
the world, to abstain from sinful desires, which war
against your soul.

1 Peter 2:11

...The words that I speak to you are spirit, and they are life.

John 6:63

6 -Speaking God's Word can inspire us to rise up and do great things.

Countless inspirational leaders have changed the course of history with words. Hope filled words can lift spirits to do the seemingly impossible. Coaches have inspired weak teams to victory with faith words. Presidents have lifted the spirit of a nation with words. Sick people have battled on with words of hope. We need to stir up our own faith with words of faith and build ourselves up.

> *But you, dear friends, must build each other up in your most holy faith, pray in the power of the Holy Spirit, and await the mercy of our Lord Jesus Christ, who will bring you eternal life. In this way, you will keep yourselves safe in God's love.*

Jude 1:20-21

7-Speaking God's Word can restore our joy.

With negativity pervading this world, it is easy to lose the joy that the Spirit brings us. Christians need that joy; it is our strength. Joy makes us want to shout from the mountain tops God's goodness. Oh, the joy of just thinking it is possible to have joy again! When did you last feel joy? God's words and praise can lift us up from very dark places to those places of joy and peace like nothing else can.

> *Your words were found, and I ate them, And Your word was to me the joy and rejoicing of my heart; For I am called by Your name, O LORD God of hosts.*

Jeremiah 15:16

47

8-Speaking God's truths helps us resist the temptations of the enemy.

Our flesh is constantly plagued with temptations. We need to flee from them physically and mentally. Even Jesus spoke God's scripture to resist the temptations of Satan.

And the devil said to Him, "If You are the Son of God, command this stone to become bread." But Jesus answered him, saying, "It is written, 'Man shall not live by bread alone, but by every word of God.'"

Luke 4:3-4

And they overcame him by the blood of the Lamb and by the word of their testimony, and they did not love their lives to the death.

Revelation 12:11

9-Speaking God's truths brings peace.

Guess what happens when you speak God's promises. Your mind stays focused on God and positive uplifting things that bring us "God peace." Isaiah said:

You will keep him in perfect peace, Whose mind is stayed on You, Because he trusts in You.

Isaiah 26:3

10-Speaking and believing God's Word is healing.

My son, pay attention to what I say; listen closely to my words. Do not let them out of your sight, keep them within your heart; for they are life to those who find them and health to a man's whole body.

Proverbs 4:20-22

He sent forth his word and healed them; he rescued them from the grave.

Psalm 107:20

There is one who speaks like the piercings of a sword, But the tongue of the wise promotes health.

Proverbs 12:18

The light of the eyes rejoices the heart, And a good report makes the bones healthy.

Proverbs 15:30

Pleasant words are like a honeycomb, Sweetness to the soul and health to the bones.

Proverbs 16:24

Do you think speaking out God's promises about healing would be a good report and sweetness to our souls? You Bet! "Well, the doctor said this ... "" Well, my God says this... and I live by faith not by sight! I believe in you, Jesus, and You are my healer."

Go ahead and believe in miracles and that you are worthy through His blood. Isn't one of God's names - Jehova Rapha – "the God who heals"? Well, I believe, and obviously Jesus did too, that it is His will to heal. We need to remember that we have authority over the devil and his sicknesses and can speak a word, and the demon of infirmity must flee. We can be forgiven through confession and we have been redeemed from the curse . Jesus said by their faith they were healed. And we were healed by the stripes of Jesus. It is time for his body to be more than conquerors and speak the truth of the good news and proclaim our VICTORY so we can be effective for the kingdom! Let's ONLY BELIEVE in this magnificent gospel and His great love for us!

And behold, a leper came to him and knelt before him, saying, "Lord, if you will, you can make me clean."

49

And Jesus stretched out his hand and touched him, saying, "I will; be clean." And immediately his leprosy was cleansed.

Matthew 8:2-3

But thanks be to God, who gives us the victory through our Lord Jesus Christ.

1Corinthians 15:57

Can our faith in Jesus make us well?

And suddenly, a woman who had a flow of blood for twelve years came from behind and touched the hem of His garment. For she said to herself, "If only I may touch His garment, I shall be made well." But Jesus turned around, and when He saw her He said, "Be of good cheer, daughter; your faith has made you well." And the woman was made well from that hour.

Matthew 9:20-22

Then Jesus said to him, "Go your way; your faith has made you well." And immediately he received his sight and followed Jesus on the road.

Mark 10:52

And He said to him, "Arise, go your way. Your faith has made you well."

Luke 17:19

Remember, faith in God comes by hearing and hearing the word of God; meditating on and speaking God's word will cause our faith to rise up, and we will become overcomers of the temptations of the world, our flesh, and the enemy. I believe if we would at least begin to speak it, even though we may not have that kind of faith in our hearts at the moment, hearing it will cause our minds to think on it. Our inner man will be strengthened, and faith will rise up over time. Our minds will begin to be renewed. We will begin to envision what the victory looks like (our body healed, our child as a Christian, our bills paid, our job secured) and to believe truth instead of the bad reports. How do we overcome the world? Through our faith we overcome. Obviously we speak in combination with the other aspects of our Christian walk: reading and meditating on God's Word, praying, receiving the Holy Spirit, seeking first His kingdom and obeying His Word.

11 – Speaking God's Word helps us to begin living by faith in Him and not by sight. (remember the crashing waves)

God wants us to stop looking at the natural situation and focus on Him, His will, and His kingdom. The enemy wants us to look at the dire circumstances and doubt God's abilities. The devil wants us to be scared. He wants us to be intimidated. He wants us to speak our doom and despair. That way he can drown us with the wind and waves (as when Peter lost focus on Jesus). Faith doesn't guess it will happen; faith knows and speaks those things that are not as though they already are.

By faith we understand that the worlds were framed by the word of God, so that the things which are seen were not made of things which are visible.

Hebrews 11:3

So we are always confident, knowing that while we are at home in the body we are absent from the Lord. For we walk by faith, not by sight.

2 Corinthians 5:6-7

12 -Speaking God's truths can help us turn into that new creation...

Sometimes, speaking God's truths may be hard because it may totally contradict our very personalities and attitudes that have defined us for many years. You know, when we have become those whining Willys, nagging Nancys, downer Debbies, gossiping Glendas, hopeless Harrys, fearful Freddies, or judgemental Janes. Bringing the light of God's Word into our hearts will be healing to our souls; we will begin to emanate life towards others, instead of draining the life from others.

Let no corrupt word proceed out of your mouth, but what is good for necessary edification, that it may impart grace to the hearers. And do not grieve the Holy Spirit of God, by whom you were sealed for the day of redemption. Let all bitterness, wrath, anger, clamor, and evil speaking be put away from you, with all malice.

Ephesians 4:29-31

But I tell you that men will have to give account on the Day of Judgment for every careless word they have spoken. For by your words you will be acquitted, and by your words you will be condemned."

Matthew 12:36 -37

13- Praise and thanksgiving can bring miracles and put an end to depression.

I cannot say enough about the positive effects of singing praises out loud about what our God has done for us! There are over 250 scriptures speaking about praise. I believe God is letting us know that praise is a mighty weapon to overcome the torment of the enemy. When we begin praising and thanking God with our mouths, we are raised above the circumstances; faith flows into the atmosphere; the enemy is stopped in his tracks, and our minds cannot stay depressed or negative. God inhabits the praises of His people. When that anointing comes, healings are manifested. When we praise, our inner man is built up, joy comes, and depression leaves.

How did Paul sing praises in prison? No doubt, the average human could have found himself in fear, depression, and hopelessness. But Paul kept his eyes on Jesus. He kept his eternal perspective in the midst of dire circumstance and believed! Is this not an example that we should follow?

O my Strength, I will watch and give heed to You and sing praises; for God is my Defense (my Protector and High Tower).

Psalm 59:9 Amp

To console those who mourn in Zion, To give them beauty for ashes, The oil of joy for mourning, The garment of praise for the spirit of heaviness; That they may be called trees of righteousness, The planting of the LORD, that He may be glorified."

Isaiah 61:3

Sing to God, sing praises to His name; Extol Him who rides on the clouds, By His name YAH, And rejoice before Him.

Psalm 68:4

Let my mouth be filled with Your praise And with Your glory all the day.

Psalm 71:8

53

14- Speaking God's Word puts righteousness and the power of life back on our tongue.

What did God say to think about and speak about? Righteous things. We cannot go wrong singing praise songs and speaking scripture.

> *Yes, my inmost being will rejoice when your lips speak right things.*
>
> Proverbs 23:16

> *It is the Spirit who gives life; the flesh profits nothing. The words that I speak to you are spirit, and they are life.*
>
> John 6:63

15 – Speaking God's Word can release angels to work on our situations.

If you were in a dire situation, wouldn't it be nice to know that angels could be sent to minister on your behalf? The Bible says they are. Now suppose you spoke out and said, "Thank You, Lord, that I have angels to work on my behalf. Thank You that You love me and that by Jesus' stripes I was healed! Thank You that I have victory through Christ, and that no weapon formed against me shall prosper; even though the enemy meant harm, you will turn it around for good because I love You!" The angels could work with that because you are prophesying God's will and Word over your life; angels help to bring God's Word to pass.

> *Praise the LORD, you his angels, you mighty ones who do his bidding, who obey his word.*
>
> Psalm103:20

Are they not all ministering spirits sent forth to minister for those who will inherit salvation?

Hebrews 1:14

Then Jesus said to him, "Away with you, Satan! For it is written, 'You shall worship the LORD your God, and Him only you shall serve.'" Then the devil left Him, and behold, angels came and ministered to Him.

Matthew 4:10-11

And the smoke of the incense, with the prayers of the saints, ascended before God from the angel's hand.

Revelation 8:4

Then he said to me, "Do not fear, Daniel, for from the first day that you set your heart to understand, and to humble yourself before your God, your words were heard; and I have come because of your words. But the prince of the kingdom of Persia withstood me twenty-one days; and behold, Michael, one of the chief princes, came to help me, for I had been left alone there with the kings of Persia.

Daniel 10: 12-13

I will say of the LORD, "He is my refuge and my fortress, my God, in whom I trust...then no harm will befall you, no disaster will come near your tent. For he will command his angels concerning you to guard you in all your ways;

Psalm 91:2, 10-11

Do you think I cannot call on my Father, and he will at once put at my disposal more than twelve legions of angels?

Matthew 26:53

Now suppose you were in a dire situation and didn't pray with thanksgiving but grumbled to your neighbor and spoke the words, "I don't know what God is doing. I prayed, but nothing happened. This is the third time this year, and I'm tired of it. I guess maybe he's trying to teach me a lesson. I'm feeling so sick. I guess I'll be bed ridden for a week now and lose more income."

Now suppose the angels were waiting there to work on your behalf and then those words were spoken. I believe they would be stopped by those words because the prayer of faith, not unbelief, shall heal the sick. An angel is not going to work with words that contradict God's Word. The scripture says that a fool's mouth is his destruction. We should put tape over a grumbling mouth. I believe demons wait to see what we believe or not by listening to our mouths. They can use our mouths and lack of faith to bring forth Satan's agenda. Remember, Satan seeks whom he may devour. He can devour anyone in fear and doubt, and will gladly oblige us when we are in unbelief and are speaking death over our lives.

> *"Also I say to you, whoever confesses Me before men, him the Son of Man also will confess before the angels of God. But he who denies Me before men will be denied before the angels of God. "*
>
> Luke 12:8-9

> *Later Jesus found him at the temple and said to him, "See, you are well again. Stop sinning or something worse may happen to you."*
>
> John 5:14

> *A fool's mouth is his destruction, And his lips are the snare of his soul.*
>
> Proverbs 18:7

> *Jesus called the crowd to him and said, "Listen and understand. What goes into a man's mouth does not make him 'unclean,' but what comes out of his mouth, that is what makes him 'unclean.' "*
>
> Matthew 15:10-11

So they were offended at Him. But Jesus said to them, "A prophet is not without honor except in his own country and in his own house." Now He did not do many mighty works there because of their unbelief.

Matthew 13:57-58

But when He had turned around and looked at His disciples, He rebuked Peter, saying, "Get behind Me, Satan! For you are not mindful of the things of God, but the things of men."

Mark 8:33

But Peter said, "Ananias, why has Satan filled your heart to lie to the Holy Spirit and keep back part of the price of the land for yourself? While it remained, was it not your own? And after it was sold, was it not in your own control? Why have you conceived this thing in your heart? You have not lied to men but to God."

Acts 5:3-4

Then one of the twelve, called Judas Iscariot, went to the chief priests and said, "What are you willing to give me if I deliver Him to you?" And they counted out to him thirty pieces of silver.

Matthew 26:14-15

... And having dipped the bread, He gave it to Judas Iscariot, the son of Simon. Now after the piece of bread, Satan entered him. Then Jesus said to him, "What you do, do quickly."

John 13:26-27

16 – Speaking God's Word to, and over, our children is prophesying blessing over them and giving them a direction in which to follow.

Blessing children was an important practice in the Bible. God blessed His children as well. Why do we not speak blessing out over our children? Instead of prophesying defeat over them, what if we spoke God's blessing of what He has called them to be? Go ahead, look at your teenage child and say, "I thank God that He is perfecting those things concerning you, and that you are becoming a strong man/woman of God and fulfilling your purpose that He had for you since the beginning of time."

> *And the LORD spoke to Moses, saying: "Speak to Aaron and his sons, saying, 'This is the way you shall bless the children of Israel. Say to them: "The LORD bless you and keep you; The LORD make His face shine upon you, And be gracious to you; The LORD lift up His countenance upon you, And give you peace."'*

Numbers 6:22-26

> *Then the word of the LORD came to me, saying: "Before I formed you in the womb I knew you; before you were born I sanctified you; I ordained you a prophet to the nations."*
> *Then said I: "Ah, Lord GOD! Behold, I cannot speak, for I am a youth." But the LORD said to me: "Do not say, 'I am a youth,...*

Jeremiah 1:4-7

> *For I know the thoughts that I think toward you, says the LORD, thoughts of peace and not of evil, to give you a future and a hope.*

Jeremiah 29:11

The Lord will perfect that which concerns me; Your
mercy and loving-kindness,...

Psalm 138:8

And he brought them out and said, "Sirs, what must I
do to be saved?" So they said, "Believe on the Lord
Jesus Christ, and you will be saved, you and your
household." Then they spoke the word of the Lord to
him and to all who were in his house.

Acts 16:30-32

17 – Speaking God's truths is a testimony and witness to the world of God's goodness.

Go ahead and put your mouth where your faith is. In love, do not be ashamed to speak out God's word in a crooked and depraved generation. They need to hear and see what this loving God can do.

For whoever is ashamed of Me and My words, of him
the Son of Man will be ashamed when He comes in
His own glory, and in His Father's, and of the holy
angels.

Luke 9:26

And since we have the same spirit of faith, according
to what is written, "I believed and therefore I spoke,"
we also believe and therefore speak,...

2 Corinthians 4:13

Oh, give thanks to the LORD! Call upon His name;
Make known His deeds among the peoples! Sing to
Him, sing psalms to Him; Talk of all His wondrous
works!

Psalm 105:1-2

18 - Speaking God's Word in your prayers assures that you are praying His will.

If anyone does not remain in me, he is like a branch that is thrown away and withers; such branches are picked up, thrown into the fire and burned. If you remain in me and my words remain in you, ask whatever you wish, and it will be given you.

John 15:6-7

Now this is the confidence that we have in Him, that if we ask anything according to His will, He hears us. And if we know that He hears us, whatever we ask, we know that we have the petitions that we have asked of Him.

1 John 15:14-15

19 – Speaking His Word helps us abide in that Word and that sets us free.

Obeying God's word can literally set us free from the bondages of sin in our flesh and help us to live free in the spirit.

Then Jesus said to those Jews who believed Him, "If you abide in My word, you are My disciples indeed. And you shall know the truth, and the truth shall make you free."

John 8:31-32

It is the Spirit who gives life; the flesh profits nothing. The words that I speak to you are spirit, and they are life. But there are some of you who do not believe."

John 6:63-64

9

How often should we speak, utter, pray, or sing life words with our tongue?

Let's just put it this way: we can't do it too much. The world bombards us all day long with negativity; the enemy whispers doubt and fear often. We need to hear God's word more than we hear the world's fear. We need to build ourselves up. We should be listening to God programs on TV and radio and hearing praise and worship in our car and be speaking God's truths as many times a day as we can, especially if fighting a battle. It holds the power of life instead of death over our situations. Joshua said:

> *This Book of the Law shall not depart from your mouth, but you shall meditate in it day and night, that you may observe to do according to all that is written in it. For then you will make your way prosperous, and then you will have good success.*
>
> Joshua 1:8

It sounds like God wanted us to speak and meditate on his word day and night and never let it depart from our mouths. I picture every time we speak God's word, our shield just extinguished another fiery dart of the enemy's. God's word is the best and cheapest medicine, armor, joy maker, peace bringer, happy drug, and enemy destroyer you can use.

10

Practical Examples:

The following examples show how you can take the truths of scripture and personalize them to speak life over yourself.

Instead of saying, "I'm always broke," we could speak a blessing and say, "My God is able to do exceedingly and abundantly above all that I ask or think, according to the power that works in me; to Him be glory! You became poor so I could be rich. You are Jehovah Jireh, my Provider! The Lord is my shepherd, I shall not want!"

Instead of yielding to returning symptoms of sickness, would we dare to say, "Satan you are a liar. It is written, 'By Jesus' stripes I have been healed.' Jesus redeemed me from any genetic curse by becoming a curse for me. Through Jesus, I have life and life more abundantly. I praise You, God, for Your goodness and mercy to me. I praise You that I was healed two-thousand years ago. I confess my sins and they are forgiven. Thank You, God, that Your will be done on earth as it is in Heaven: there is no sickness in Heaven. You raised the dead, You healed the sick; surely my problem is not too big for You. You are Jehovah Rapha, my God Who heals!"?

Instead of saying, "I will never beat this addiction," speak life over the situation and dare to say, "I confess this and I thank You, Lord, that you have cleansed me from all unrighteousness. My mind is renewed to truth and the truth has set me free! I desire You over cigarettes or anything else in my life! You have given me everything I need to live a life of Godliness and holiness, and I can do all things through Christ who strengthens me!"

Instead of letting the tormenting demon of fear and anxiety wreak havoc in your life, you could pick up your sword and speak, "Satan, Jesus has given me authority over you and your demons. I command you right now, Spirit of fear, to leave me and don't ever come back. God has not given me a spirit of fear, but one of power, of love, and of a sound mind. I praise you, Father, for giving me peace and peace that surpasses all understanding, for I keep my mind stayed on you." Building your faith up by declaring His promises will begin to drown out fear.

Instead of accepting debt and the curse of never being able to get on top, say to the enemy who comes to steal, kill, and destroy, "I break your curse of poverty over me, enemy. My sins from the past have been forgiven. Jesus redeemed me from the curse. Jesus, I open my heart to You to heal me of past wounds. I have victory and strength to do all that I need to do and to change my patterns through Christ Jesus. I will seek first His kingdom and His righteousness, and all these things shall be added unto me!"

Instead of flopping back into bed with symptoms of the flu, battle the ugly viruses! Say, "The joy of the Lord is my strength! I rebuke you fever. I curse you, virus, to shrivel up and die. You are not producing good fruit. I am redeemed from the curse because Jesus became a curse for me. I am not weak, but I am strong."

Instead of going another year unable to forgive someone who has hurt you deeply, pray to God, saying, "Lord, I thank You that You forgave me when I was a sinner; therefore, I forgive this person who has hurt me. You said to pray for those who spitefully use me and bless those who curse me, so I pray that You bless "so and so" and draw their hearts unto You for salvation. Thank You that You will give me the words to speak when I am around them. Strengthen my inner man that it will not be weak against their abuses. I repent of my unforgiveness. My self-worth is found in You, for I am a child of the most high God and a joint heir with Jesus!"

"How can I speak of things that haven't happened yet?"

Remember that God said to let the redeemed of the Lord say so! And He said in Joel, "Let the weak say I am strong!" God changed

Abram's name to "father of many nations" before he even had a son. There is no time with God. In God's eyes, it was already done two-thousand years ago. Go ahead and prophesy and pray. Thank Him for the promises that He has already given us; the same promises that Satan wants to steal from us through doubt.

By faith we understand that the worlds were framed by the word of God, so that the things which are seen were not made of things which are visible.

Hebrews 11:3

Though now you do not see Him, yet believing, you rejoice with joy inexpressible and full of glory, receiving the end of your faith—the salvation of your souls.

1 Peter 1:8-9

(as it is written, "I have made you a father of many nations") in the presence of Him whom he believed— God, who gives life to the dead and calls those things which do not exist as though they did;

Romans 4:17

Thou shalt also decree a thing, and it shall be established unto thee: and the light shall shine upon thy ways.

Job 22:28 KJV

11

Scriptures For Our Use

Out of the overflow of the heart, our mouths will speak.

Below are just a few of the many scriptures you can meditate on to fill your heart up with the truths of God. Then, from the overflow of your heart, your mouth will speak the promises of God, instead of doubt and fear.

Life words for peace:

Be anxious for nothing, but in everything by prayer and supplication, with thanksgiving, let your requests be made known to God; and the peace of God, which surpasses all understanding, will guard your hearts and minds through Christ Jesus.

Philippians 4:6-7

Come to Me, all you who labor and are heavy laden, and I will give you rest. Take My yoke upon you and learn from Me, for I am gentle and lowly in heart, and you will find rest for your souls.

Matthew 11:28-29

These things I have spoken to you, that in Me you may have peace. In the world you will have tribulation; but be of good cheer, I have overcome the world."

John 16:33

Take My yoke upon you and learn from Me, for I am gentle and lowly in heart, and you will find rest for your souls.

Matthew 11:29

You will keep him in perfect peace, Whose mind is stayed on You, Because he trusts in You.

Isaiah 26 :3

Life words for our children:

The righteous man walks in his integrity; His children are blessed after him.

Proverbs 20:7

They shall not labor in vain, Nor bring forth children for trouble; For they shall be the descendants of the blessed of the LORD, And their offspring with them.

Isaiah 65:23

For I know the thoughts that I think toward you, says the LORD, thoughts of peace and not of evil, to give you a future and a hope.

Jeremiah 29 :11

The Lord will perfect that which concerns me; Your mercy and loving-kindness,...

Psalm 138:8

And he brought them out and said, "Sirs, what must I do to be saved?" So they said, "Believe on the Lord Jesus Christ, and you will be saved, you and your household." Then they spoke the word of the Lord to him and to all who were in his house.

Acts 16:30-32

Life words for healing:

Praise the LORD, O my soul; all my inmost being, praise his holy name. Praise the LORD, O my soul, and forget not all his benefits- who forgives all your sins and heals all your diseases,...

Psalm 103:1-3

*The LORD is near to those who have a broken heart,
And saves such as have a contrite spirit. Many are
the afflictions of the righteous, But the LORD deliv-
ers him out of them all. He guards all his bones; Not
one of them is broken.*

Psalm 34:18-20

*...who Himself bore our sins in His own body on the
tree, that we, having died to sins, might live for righteousness—by whose stripes you were healed.*

1 Peter 2:24

Life words when we are in doubt:

*He who did not spare His own Son, but delivered Him
up for us all, how shall He not with Him also freely
give us all things?*

Romans 8:32

*Jesus said to him, "If you can believe, all things are
possible to him who believes."*

Mark 9:23

*Jesus said to him, "Thomas, because you have seen
Me, you have believed. Blessed are those who have
not seen and yet have believed."*

John 20:29

Life words for financial issues:

*And my God shall supply all your need according to
His riches in glory by Christ Jesus.*

Philippians 4:19

*But seek first the kingdom of God and His righteous-
ness, and all these things shall be added to you.
Therefore do not worry about tomorrow, for tomorrow*

69

will worry about its own things. Sufficient for the day is its own trouble.

Matthew 6:33-34

Remember this: Whoever sows sparingly will also reap sparingly, and whoever sows generously will also reap generously.

2 Corinthians 9:6

And God is able to make all grace abound to you, so that in all things at all times, having all that you need, you will abound in every good work. As it is written: "He has scattered abroad his gifts to the poor; his righteousness endures forever." Now he who supplies seed to the sower and bread for food will also supply and increase your store of seed and will enlarge the harvest of your righteousness. You will be made rich in every way so that you can be generous on every occasion,...

2 Corinthians 9:8-11

Now to Him who is able to do exceedingly abundantly above all that we ask or think, according to the power that works in us, to Him be glory...

Ephesians 3:20-21

For you know the grace of our Lord Jesus Christ, that though He was rich, yet for your sakes He became poor, that you through His poverty might become rich.

2 Corinthians 8:9

Life words for a troubled marriage:

Let the husband render to his wife the affection due her, and likewise also the wife to her husband. The wife does not have authority over her own body, but the husband does. And likewise the husband does not

70

have authority over his own body, but the wife does.

1Corinthians 7:3-4

Let nothing be done through selfish ambition or conceit, but in lowliness of mind let each esteem others better than himself. Let each of you look out not only for his own interests, but also for the interests of others.

Philippians 2:3-4

Wives, likewise, be submissive to your own husbands, that even if some do not obey the word, they, without a word, may be won by the conduct of their wives, when they observe your chaste conduct accompanied by fear. Do not let your adornment be merely outward—arranging the hair, wearing gold, or putting on fine apparel— rather let it be the hidden person of the heart, with the incorruptible beauty of a gentle and quiet spirit, which is very precious in the sight of God. For in this manner, in former times, the holy women who trusted in God also adorned themselves, being submissive to their own husbands, as Sarah obeyed Abraham, calling him lord, whose daughters you are if you do good and are not afraid with any terror.

1Peter3:1-6

Finally, all of you be of one mind, having compassion for one another; love as brothers, be tenderhearted, be courteous; not returning evil for evil or reviling for reviling, but on the contrary blessing, knowing that you were called to this, that you may inherit a blessing. For "He who would love life And see good days, Let him refrain his tongue from evil, And his lips from speaking deceit.

1Peter3:8-10

In Closing . . .

God has told us so many amazing things about who we are and what we have in Christ. He loves us so much and wants us to be overcomers. All His words are words He gave us to help us. Even though the enemy has tried to trap us through lies and doubts, I believe God wants us to begin seeing ourselves and our situations through His eyes - to be more like David. I believe speaking His word would help ward off the enemy before he strikes and defeat the enemy during an assult. Watching what we say, is just one small thing we can begin practicing to help our walk become stronger, and to help us become those people of faith – overcomers – more than conquerors; believers and doers of the word.

Remember:

Words kill, words give life; they're either poison or fruit—you choose.

Proverbs 18:21 TMT

I call heaven and earth as witnesses today against you, that I have set before you life and death, blessing and cursing; therefore choose life, that both you and your descendants may live; that you may love the LORD your God, that you may obey His voice, and that you may cling to Him, for He is your life and the length of your days;...

Deuteronomy 30:19-20

26/11/95

30971222R00044

Made in the USA
Lexington, KY
25 March 2014